SURVIVING THE AI REVOLUTION

A Guide to the Professions at Risk

Nathaniel Haselton

Haselton Media Group

"It is not the strongest of the species that survives, nor the most intelligent that survives. It is the one that is the most adaptable to change."

CHARLES DARWIN

CONTENTS

Welcome to this book on the top professions that are expected to be impacted by AI and how to adapt. As artificial intelligence (AI) continues to advance at an unprecedented pace, it is becoming increasingly clear that many jobs and industries will undergo significant changes in the coming years. The purpose of this book is to provide insights into which professions are likely to be impacted the most by AI and how individuals in those professions can prepare themselves for the changes to come.

The book will begin by providing an overview of the current state of AI and its potential impact on the job market. We will explore the different types of AI, such as machine learning, natural language processing, and robotics, and how they are already being used in various industries.

The following chapters will then focus on specific professions that are expected to be impacted by AI, such as customer service representatives, financial analysts, lawyers, doctors, and truck drivers, among others. We will examine the tasks and skills that these professions involve, and how they may be automated or transformed by AI.

The book will also explore the new job opportunities that may arise as a result of AI, such as AI trainers, explainers, and maintainers, and how individuals can position themselves for these roles.

Finally, the book will provide practical advice on how individuals can adapt to the changes brought about by AI. We will discuss strategies for upskilling and reskilling, networking and building a personal brand, and leveraging online platforms and resources to stay ahead of the curve.

Overall, this book aims to provide a comprehensive guide for individuals who want to understand how AI is transforming the job market and how they can prepare themselves for the future. Whether you are a student, a mid-career professional, or a business owner, this book will offer insights and practical advice to help you stay ahead in the age of AI. Artificial intelligence has the potential to automate or augment many occupations, which could lead to some job displacement or obsolescence. Here are some examples of occupations that may be at risk:

1. Data entry clerks and related occupations

2. Telemarketers and customer service representatives

3. Bookkeepers, accounting clerks, and auditors

4. Financial analysts and advisors

5. Insurance underwriters and claims adjusters

6. Tax preparers and income tax return preparers

7. Radiologists and other medical imaging professionals

8. Loan officers and credit analysts

9. Market research analysts and marketing specialists

10. Computer programmers and software developers

11. . Retail salespeople and cashiers

12. Fast food workers

13. Fast food workers and other food preparation and serving occupations

14. Manufacturing assembly line workers

15. Customer support and technical support specialists

It is important to note that the impact of AI on employment varies by industry and occupation, and some jobs may be more resistant to automation than others. Additionally, the adoption of AI technologies may create new job opportunities in areas such as AI development, maintenance, and integration. Therefore, it is difficult to predict which specific jobs may become obsolete in the future, but it is clear that the workforce will need to adapt and develop new skills to remain competitive in an AI-driven economy.

THE CURRENT STATE OF AI

Artificial Intelligence (AI) is an umbrella term used to describe the ability of machines to perform tasks that would typically require human intelligence, such as learning, problem-solving, and decision-making. AI has made significant strides in recent years, and its potential impact on the job market is a topic of much debate.

Currently, AI technologies are being used in a variety of industries, from finance and healthcare to manufacturing and retail. These technologies are being used to automate many routine and repetitive tasks, freeing up human workers to focus on more creative and complex work. Additionally, AI is being used to enhance decision-making in areas such as customer service and risk assessment.

However, the rise of AI has also raised concerns about its potential impact on the job market. Some experts argue that AI could lead to significant job losses, particularly in industries where routine and repetitive tasks are prevalent. For example, the adoption of AI in manufacturing could lead to the displacement of workers in assembly line jobs. Similarly, the use of AI in customer service could lead to the displacement of workers in call centers.

On the other hand, other experts argue that AI could create new job opportunities, particularly in areas such as data analysis and software engineering. These jobs would require a different set of skills than those currently required for many routine and repetitive jobs, and workers would need to be retrained to acquire these skills.

Overall, the impact of AI on the job market remains uncertain. While some industries are likely to experience significant job losses due to the adoption of AI, others may see new job opportunities emerge. The key to managing the impact of AI on the job market will be to invest in education and training programs to help workers acquire the skills they need to succeed in a changing job market.n and training programs to help workers acquire the skills they need to succeed in a changing job market.

Currently, AI is being used in a variety of applications, including:

Natural language processing (NLP): NLP refers to the ability of machines to understand and interpret human language. NLP is being used in applications such as chatbots, virtual assistants, and voice recognition technology.

Machine learning (ML): ML involves the use of algorithms and statistical models to enable machines to learn from data and improve their performance over time. ML is being used in applications such as image recognition, predictive analytics, and recommendation systems.

Robotics: Robotics involves the use of machines to perform tasks that would typically require human intervention. Robotics is being used in applications such as manufacturing, healthcare, and agriculture.

Autonomous vehicles: Autonomous vehicles are vehicles that can operate without human intervention. Autonomous vehicles are being developed for use in transportation and logistics, and they have the potential to revolutionize the way goods and people are moved around the world.

Computer vision: Computer vision involves the ability of machines to interpret and understand visual information. Computer vision is being used in applications such as facial recognition, object detection, and surveillance systems.

While AI has the potential to bring significant benefits to society, such as improved efficiency, increased productivity, and better decision-making, it also poses significant challenges, such as job displacement, ethical considerations, and cyber security risks.

Therefore, it is crucial to continue to invest in research and development to ensure that AI is developed in a way that maximizes its benefits while minimizing its risks. Additionally, policymakers, industry leaders, and academics must work together to address the social and ethical implications of AI and to develop policies and regulations that ensure its responsible use. Let's look at the top professions expected to be effected by AI.

1. DATA ENTRY CLERKS

Data entry clerks and related occupations involve entering and processing data into computer systems, databases, spreadsheets, or other software applications. With the increasing use of AI technologies, such as optical character recognition (OCR) and natural language processing (NLP), data entry tasks can be automated, reducing the need for human labor.

In particular, OCR technology can scan and digitize documents such as forms, invoices, and receipts, making it faster and more accurate to extract data from them compared to manual data entry. NLP can also be used to automatically extract information from text-based sources such as emails, social media, and news articles.

As a result, the demand for data entry clerks and related occupations may decline as AI technologies become more prevalent. However, it is important to note that some data entry tasks may require human input and judgment, such as verifying and correcting errors, interpreting complex data, and performing quality control checks.

Furthermore, the adoption of AI technologies may create new job opportunities for individuals who can operate and maintain the technology, as well as those who can analyze and interpret the data generated by the technology. Therefore, while data entry clerks and related occupations may be at risk of obsolescence due to AI, individuals in these fields can prepare for the future by developing new skills such as data analysis, programming, and machine learning.

2. TELEMARKETERS AND CUSTOMER SERVICE REPRESENTATIVES

are two occupations that involve interacting with customers over the phone or online. Telemarketers typically make unsolicited calls to promote products or services, while customer service representatives handle inquiries, complaints, and other issues related to a company's products or services.

Both of these occupations require strong communication skills, as well as the ability to work under pressure and deal with potentially difficult or irate customers. In recent years, however, advances in AI and automation technology have begun to impact these roles as well.

Automated chatbots and virtual assistants are now being used to handle many customer service inquiries, while telemarketing calls are increasingly being replaced by targeted digital marketing campaigns. This shift has led to concerns about job loss and the future of work, as machines are able to perform many of these tasks more efficiently than humans.

However, some experts argue that these changes may actually

create new opportunities for workers with more specialized skills, such as data analysis and digital marketing strategy. Additionally, the human touch and empathy provided by customer service representatives is still highly valued by many consumers, and may be difficult to fully replicate with AI and automation technology.

Ultimately, the fate of telemarketers and customer service representatives remains uncertain. What is clear, however, is that technological advancements will continue to reshape the world of work in ways that are both exciting and challenging.

3. BOOKKEEPING & ACCOUNTING

AI is already transforming the way bookkeeping, accounting, and auditing tasks are performed. Many routine and repetitive tasks that were once performed by humans can now be automated using AI and machine learning algorithms.

For example, bookkeeping tasks such as data entry, invoice processing, and reconciling bank statements can be easily automated using software that utilizes OCR (optical character recognition: Optical character recognition, commonly known as OCR, is a technology that enables computers to read and interpret text from images or scanned documents. OCR software uses algorithms to analyze the patterns and shapes of characters in an image and then converts them into machine-readable text. This technology is commonly used to digitize and automate the processing of printed or handwritten text, such as in document management, data entry, and translation applications. OCR technology has made significant advancements in recent years, with high accuracy rates and the ability to recognize a wide variety of languages and writing styles.) And machine learning technologies. This can help reduce errors and save time for bookkeepers and accounting clerks.

Similarly, AI can assist in auditing tasks by automatically analyzing financial data and identifying potential errors or irregularities. This can help auditors to focus on high-risk areas and provide more comprehensive and accurate audits.

Furthermore, AI-powered software can provide real-time financial insights and reporting, enabling businesses to make informed decisions based on up-to-date information.

While the adoption of AI in these fields is still in its early stages, it's clear that AI will continue to play an increasingly important role in automating routine tasks and improving the efficiency and accuracy of bookkeeping, accounting, and auditing processes. However, it's important to note that human expertise and judgment will still be needed for more complex tasks, such as financial analysis and strategic decision-making.

4. FINANCIAL ANALYSTS AND ADVISORS

How AI is poised to replace financial analysts and advisors is a topic of debate in the industry. While AI can assist in analyzing financial data and identifying patterns, trends, and insights, there are still areas where human expertise and judgment are critical.

AI can help financial analysts and advisors to process and analyze large amounts of data quickly and accurately, providing insights and recommendations based on historical data and trends. AI can also assist in portfolio management, risk assessment, and asset allocation by analyzing market data and making predictions based on algorithms.

However, financial analysis and advice often involve complex decision-making that requires a combination of technical knowledge, strategic thinking, and interpersonal skills. These are areas where AI may fall short, as it lacks the ability to take into account the nuances of human behavior, emotions, and motivations.

Furthermore, financial analysis and advice require trust and confidence between the advisor and the client. Many clients may still prefer to work with a human advisor who can offer personalized advice and build relationships based on trust and rapport.

In conclusion, while AI can certainly assist in the work of financial analysts and advisors, it's unlikely to completely replace them in the near future. Instead, the role of AI is likely to evolve to one of a complementary tool that enhances the capabilities of human analysts and advisors, rather than replacing them altogether.

5. INSURANCE UNDERWRITERS AND CLAIMS ADJUSTERS

AI is already transforming the insurance industry by automating many tasks that were once performed by underwriters and claims adjusters.

AI can assist in risk assessment and underwriting by analyzing vast amounts of data and identifying patterns and trends that human underwriters may miss. This can help insurance companies to make more accurate pricing decisions and reduce their overall risk exposure.

Similarly, AI can assist in claims processing and adjusting by analyzing claims data and automatically flagging potentially fraudulent or inaccurate claims. This can help reduce the time and resources needed for manual claims review and improve the accuracy of claims processing.

Furthermore, AI can assist in identifying and mitigating risks, such as predicting potential losses due to natural disasters or fraud, allowing insurers to take proactive measures to minimize their exposure.

While AI can automate many routine and repetitive tasks, it's important to note that human expertise and judgment will still be needed for more complex tasks, such as negotiating settlements and handling complex claims. Additionally, the personal touch and empathy that human claims adjusters can bring to the claims process are still highly valued by customers.

In conclusion, AI is likely to play an increasingly important role in insurance underwriting and claims processing, but it's unlikely to completely replace human underwriters and claims adjusters in the near future. Instead, the role of AI is likely to evolve to one of a complementary tool that enhances the capabilities of human underwriters and adjusters, allowing them to focus on more complex and value-added tasks.

6. TAX PREPARERS

For tax preparers and income tax return preparers, the rise of AI is likely to bring about significant changes to the profession. Here are some tips to help you adapt to this change:

Focus on developing your interpersonal and communication skills - While AI can certainly assist in the processing and analysis of tax data, it lacks the ability to build relationships and communicate effectively with clients. This is where you can differentiate yourself and add value to your clients by providing personalized advice and guidance, and building long-term relationships based on trust and empathy.

Stay up-to-date with the latest AI tools and technologies - AI is rapidly evolving and improving, and staying informed about the latest tools and technologies can help you to stay ahead of the curve and remain competitive in the market. Consider investing in AI tools that can help you automate routine tasks, freeing up time for more complex tasks that require human judgment and expertise.

Embrace change and continue to learn - As with any technological disruption, it's important to embrace change and continue to learn and adapt. This may involve acquiring new skills and knowledge, such as data analytics and machine learning, to stay relevant and competitive in the market.

Focus on adding value to your clients - Ultimately, the key to success in the age of AI is to focus on adding value to your clients. This means understanding their unique needs and goals, and providing personalized advice and guidance that can help them to achieve their financial objectives.

In conclusion, while the rise of AI may bring about significant changes to the tax preparation and income tax return preparation profession, there are still plenty of opportunities to add value and differentiate yourself from the competition. By focusing on your interpersonal skills, staying up-to-date with the latest technologies, embracing change, and adding value to your clients, you can thrive in the age of AI and continue to build a successful and fulfilling career.

7. RADIOLOGISTS AND OTHER MEDICAL IMAGING PROFESSIONALS

Radiologists and other medical imaging professionals are highly skilled and specialized workers who are responsible for interpreting and analyzing medical images such as X-rays, CT scans, and MRI scans. While the rise of AI and machine learning has the potential to automate some aspects of this work, it is important to note that these technologies are not expected to fully replace radiologists and other medical imaging professionals anytime soon.

That being said, there are some ways that these professionals can adapt to the changing landscape of AI and machine learning in healthcare:

Develop new skills - As AI and machine learning become more prevalent in healthcare, radiologists and other medical imaging professionals may need to develop new skills in order to stay competitive. These might include skills in data analysis, computer science, and programming. Seek out training and development opportunities that can help you develop these skills.

Collaborate with AI tools - Rather than seeing AI as a threat, radiologists and other medical imaging professionals can collaborate with AI tools to enhance their own work. For example, AI-powered tools can help identify potential areas of concern in medical images, which can then be further analyzed and interpreted by the human radiologist.

Stay informed - Keep up-to-date with the latest developments in AI and machine learning in healthcare, and understand how they may impact your job and the industry as a whole. This will help you anticipate changes and adapt more effectively.

Focus on specialized areas - While AI may be able to perform some general tasks related to medical imaging; specialized areas such as interventional radiology or musculoskeletal radiology may require more specialized knowledge and expertise that cannot be easily automated.

Emphasize human touch - While AI and machine learning may be able to automate certain aspects of medical imaging, they cannot replace the human touch and empathy that radiologists and other medical imaging professionals bring to their work. Emphasize the importance of this human element in your work and continue to provide high-quality patient care.

Overall, the rise of AI and machine learning in healthcare is likely to have an impact on the work of radiologists and other medical imaging professionals. By developing new skills, collaborating with AI tools, staying informed, focusing on specialized areas, and emphasizing the human touch, these professionals can adapt to these changes and continue to provide high-quality patient care.

8. LOAN OFFICERS AND CREDIT ANALYSTS

Loan officers and credit analysts play a critical role in assessing and approving loans for individuals and businesses. As AI continues to evolve and become more advanced, it's likely that the role of loan officers and credit analysts will change. Here are some tips to help you adapt to this change:

Focus on developing your interpersonal and communication skills - While AI can certainly assist in the processing and analysis of loan data, it lacks the ability to build relationships and communicate effectively with clients. This is where you can differentiate yourself and add value to your clients by providing personalized advice and guidance, and building long-term relationships based on trust and empathy.

Stay up-to-date with the latest AI tools and technologies - AI is rapidly evolving and improving, and staying informed about the latest tools and technologies can help you to stay ahead of the curve and remain competitive in the market. Consider investing in AI tools that can help you automate routine tasks, freeing up time for more complex tasks that require human judgment and expertise.

Embrace change and continue to learn - As with any technological disruption, it's important to embrace change and continue to learn and adapt. This may involve acquiring new skills and knowledge, such as data analytics and machine learning, to stay relevant and competitive in the market.

Focus on adding value to your clients - Ultimately, the key to success in the age of AI is to focus on adding value to your clients. This means understanding their unique needs and goals, and providing personalized advice and guidance that can help them to achieve their financial objectives.

Emphasize your expertise and judgment - While AI can assist in the analysis of loan data, it cannot replace the expertise and judgment that loan officers and credit analysts bring to the table. Emphasize your expertise and judgment when working with clients, and demonstrate how you can add value beyond what AI can offer.

In conclusion, while the rise of AI may bring about significant changes to the loan officer and credit analyst profession, there are still plenty of opportunities to add value and differentiate yourself from the competition. By focusing on your interpersonal skills, staying up-to-date with the latest technologies, embracing change, adding value to your clients, and emphasizing your expertise and judgment, you can thrive in the age of AI and continue to build a successful and fulfilling career.

9. MARKET RESEARCH ANALYSTS AND MARKETING SPECIALISTS

Market research analysts and marketing specialists play a crucial role in helping businesses to understand their customers and target their marketing efforts. As AI continues to advance, it's important for market research analysts and marketing specialists to adapt and stay ahead of the curve. Here are some tips to help you adapt to this change:

Embrace AI as a complementary tool - While AI can certainly assist in the analysis of market data, it's important to remember that it's not a replacement for human expertise and judgment. Instead, market research analysts and marketing specialists can leverage AI as a complementary tool that enhances their ability to analyze market data and develop effective marketing strategies.

Stay up-to-date with the latest AI tools and technologies - AI is rapidly evolving and improving, and staying informed about the latest tools and technologies can help you to stay ahead of the curve and remain competitive in the market. Consider investing in AI tools that can help you to automate routine tasks, freeing up time for more complex tasks that require human judgment and expertise.

Focus on developing your unique skills and strengths - While AI can assist in the analysis of market data, it cannot replace the critical thinking and problem-solving skills that market research analysts and marketing specialists bring to the table. Focus on developing your unique skills and strengths, such as your ability to interpret market data and develop effective marketing strategies.

Emphasize your ability to provide personalized insights - While AI can certainly analyze large amounts of market data, it cannot replace the ability of market research analysts and marketing specialists to provide personalized insights that take into account the unique needs and preferences of different customer segments. Emphasize your ability to provide personalized insights when working with clients, and demonstrate how you can add value beyond what AI can offer.

Collaborate with AI technologies - One of the key benefits of AI is its ability to identify patterns and trends that may be difficult for humans to identify. Consider collaborating with AI technologies to identify these patterns and trends and use them to develop more effective marketing strategies.

In conclusion, while the rise of AI may bring about significant changes to the market research and marketing profession, there are still plenty of opportunities to add value and differentiate yourself from the competition. By embracing AI as a complementary tool, staying up-to-date with the latest technologies, focusing on developing your unique skills and strengths, emphasizing your ability to provide personalized insights, and collaborating with AI technologies, you can thrive in the age of AI and continue to provide critical support to businesses seeking to understand their customers and develop effective marketing strategies.

10. COMPUTER PROGRAMMERS AND SOFTWARE DEVELOPERS

Computer programmers and software developers are at the forefront of the AI revolution, as they are the ones who develop the algorithms and applications that power AI systems. While AI has the potential to automate many routine programming tasks, there are still many areas where human expertise and creativity are essential. Here are some tips to help computer programmers and software developers adapt to the rise of AI:

Embrace AI as a complementary tool - While AI has the potential to automate many routine programming tasks, it's important to remember that it's not a replacement for human expertise and creativity. Instead, computer programmers and software developers can leverage AI as a complementary tool that enhances their ability to develop innovative applications and solve complex problems.

Stay up-to-date with the latest AI technologies - AI is evolving rapidly, and staying informed about the latest technologies and tools can help you stay ahead of the curve and remain competitive in the industry. Consider learning new programming languages and tools that are specifically designed for developing

AI applications.

Focus on developing your unique skills and strengths - While AI may be able to automate routine tasks, it cannot replace the critical thinking, problem-solving, and creativity that computer programmers and software developers bring to the table. Focus on developing your unique skills and strengths, such as your ability to develop complex algorithms and innovative applications.

Collaborate with AI systems - Rather than seeing AI as a threat, consider collaborating with AI systems to develop more innovative applications and solutions. By working alongside AI systems, you can leverage their unique capabilities to develop new ideas and approaches that would not be possible otherwise.

Keep an open mind and be willing to learn - AI is a rapidly evolving field, and it's important to keep an open mind and be willing to learn as new technologies and approaches emerge. Stay curious and engaged with the latest developments in AI, and be willing to experiment with new tools and techniques to see what works best for your specific needs.

In conclusion, while the rise of AI may bring about significant changes to the programming and software development profession, there are still plenty of opportunities to add value and differentiate yourself from the competition. By embracing AI as a complementary tool, staying up-to-date with the latest technologies, focusing on developing your unique skills and strengths, collaborating with AI systems, and keeping an open mind and willingness to learn, you can thrive in the age of AI and continue to develop innovative applications and solutions that push the boundaries of what is possible.

11. RETAIL SALESPEOPLE AND CASHIERS

Retail salespeople and cashiers are also professions that

are likely to be impacted by the rise of AI. Here are some

tips to help them adapt to this changing landscape:

Develop new skills - As AI systems become more prevalent in retail, salespeople and cashiers need to develop new skills to stay competitive. These might include skills in digital marketing, data analysis, or customer experience design. Seek out training and development opportunities that can help you develop these skills.

Embrace technology - While AI may replace some tasks that retail salespeople and cashiers currently perform, there are also new opportunities to leverage technology to enhance your performance. For example, AI-powered tools can provide valuable insights into customer preferences and purchasing behavior, allowing you to tailor your approach and provide a better customer experience.

Focus on building relationships - While AI may be able to handle routine tasks, it cannot replace the value of human interaction and personal relationships. Focus on building strong relationships with your customers, providing personalized service, and creating a positive shopping experience that keeps them coming back.

Be adaptable - Retail is a constantly evolving industry, and it's important to be adaptable to changes in technology and customer preferences. Stay up-to-date with the latest trends and technologies, and be willing to experiment with new approaches and strategies.

Emphasize the human touch - Ultimately, the success of retail salespeople and cashiers will depend on their ability to provide a human touch that AI systems cannot replicate. Focus on developing your interpersonal skills, empathy, and problem-solving abilities, and use technology to enhance your performance rather than replace it.

In conclusion, while the rise of AI may bring about significant changes to the retail industry, there are still plenty of opportunities for salespeople and cashiers to add value and differentiate themselves from the competition. By developing new skills, embracing technology, focusing on building relationships, being adaptable, and emphasizing the human touch, you can thrive in the age of AI and continue to provide excellent service to your customers.

12.FAST FOOD WORKERS

Fast food workers and other food preparation and serving occupations have traditionally been viewed as entry-level, low-skill positions that provide a starting point for people entering the workforce. However, with the rise of AI and automation in the fast food industry, these positions are increasingly being replaced by machines.

This can have a negative impact on the American workforce and on the economy as a whole. According to a recent report by the National Bureau of Economic Research, the widespread adoption of automation technologies in the fast food industry could lead to the displacement of between 3.8 million and 7.5 million jobs in the United States.

This loss of jobs in the fast food industry could have a ripple effect throughout the economy, as many of these jobs provide a critical starting point for young workers and others who are just entering the workforce. These jobs provide an opportunity to gain valuable experience and skills, build a work history, and earn a paycheck that can be used to support further education and training.

Furthermore, the fast food industry has historically been a key driver of economic growth and job creation in the United States. According to a report by the National Restaurant Association, the restaurant industry is projected to create 1.6 million new jobs in the United States by 2030. However, the widespread adoption of automation technologies in this industry could significantly slow down this growth.

Overall, the loss of fast food jobs as an entry-level, low-skill profession could have a significant impact on American prosperity and the foundation of the American workforce. While it is important to embrace the benefits of AI and automation, it is also important to consider the potential consequences and work to ensure that the benefits are shared fairly and equitably.

13. TRUCK DRIVERS AND DELIVERY DRIVERS

Truck drivers and delivery drivers are another group of workers who are likely to be impacted by the rise of AI and autonomous vehicles. Here are some tips for adapting to this changing landscape:

Develop new skills - As AI and autonomous vehicles become more prevalent in the transportation industry, truck drivers and delivery drivers will need to develop new skills to stay competitive. These might include skills in data analysis, logistics management, or remote monitoring. Seek out training and development opportunities that can help you develop these skills.

Stay informed - Keep up-to-date with the latest developments in AI and autonomous vehicles, and understand how they may impact your job and the industry as a whole. This will help you anticipate changes and adapt more effectively.

Embrace technology - While AI and autonomous vehicles may replace some tasks that truck drivers and delivery drivers currently perform, there are also new opportunities to leverage technology to enhance your performance. For example, AI-powered route optimization tools can help you plan more efficient routes and reduce fuel costs.

Network and build relationships - As the industry changes, it's important to build relationships with other professionals and organizations in the field. Attend industry events and conferences, connect with peers on social media, and build relationships with potential employers and clients.

Consider alternative roles - While some roles in the transportation industry may be replaced by AI and autonomous vehicles, there may also be new opportunities in related areas. For example, logistics management, dispatching, and remote monitoring are all areas that may see growth as a result of these technological changes.

Overall, the rise of AI and autonomous vehicles is likely to have a significant impact on the transportation industry and on truck drivers and delivery drivers in particular. By developing new skills, staying informed, embracing technology, networking and building relationships, and considering alternative roles, you can position yourself for success in this changing landscape.

14. MANUFACTURING ASSEMBLY LINE WORKERS

Manufacturing assembly line workers are one of the professions that are expected to be impacted by AI. Assembly line work often involves repetitive tasks that can be automated with the help of robots and other forms of AI. For example, robots can be used to perform tasks such as picking and placing parts, welding, painting, and quality control.

As a result, some manufacturing jobs may be eliminated or transformed by AI. However, there are also opportunities for workers to adapt and acquire new skills to work alongside AI. For example, workers can learn how to operate and maintain the robots, or work in roles such as programming, design, or engineering of automated systems.

To prepare for the changes brought about by AI, assembly line workers can take the following steps:

Stay informed: Keep up to date with the latest advancements in AI and robotics. Follow industry news and attend relevant conferences and training programs.

Develop technical skills: Learn how to operate and maintain robots, as well as other automated systems. Gain knowledge of programming, automation, and robotics technologies.

Focus on soft skills: Aspects of work that cannot be automated, such as communication, problem-solving, and teamwork, are still important. Develop strong interpersonal skills to complement technical skills.

Upskill and reskill: Seek out training and certification programs that will enhance skills and knowledge in areas relevant to AI and automation.

Embrace change: Adopt a positive attitude towards change and be open to new opportunities that may arise as a result of AI and automation.

In summary, while AI and automation may transform the nature of manufacturing assembly line work, workers can prepare themselves by staying informed, developing technical and soft skills, upskilling and reskilling, and embracing change.

15. CUSTOMER SUPPORT AND TECHNICAL SUPPORT SPECIALISTS

Customer support and technical support specialists are also professions that are expected to be impacted by AI. Many companies are already using chatbots and virtual assistants to provide customer service and technical support to their customers.

Chatbots and virtual assistants can handle simple and routine tasks, such as answering frequently asked questions and providing basic troubleshooting guidance. This can free up human customer support and technical support specialists to focus on more complex tasks that require human intervention.

To adapt to the changes brought about by AI in customer support and technical support, specialists can take the following steps:

Develop new skills: Learn how to work with chatbots and virtual assistants and understand how they can be used to improve customer support and technical support processes. Develop skills in areas such as data analysis and machine learning, which are increasingly relevant in customer support and technical support.

Focus on complex tasks: As AI takes over routine tasks, customer support and technical support specialists can focus on more complex tasks that require human intervention, such as problem-solving, conflict resolution, and handling complex technical issues.

Build soft skills: Develop strong communication, empathy, and interpersonal skills, which are essential in providing high-quality customer support and technical support.

Learn from customer interactions: Use data analytics and AI-powered tools to gain insights into customer interactions, and identify areas for improvement in customer support and technical support processes.

Embrace AI-powered tools: Collaborate with chatbots and virtual assistants to improve customer support and technical support processes and deliver better customer experiences.

In summary, while AI and automation may transform the nature of customer support and technical support work, specialists can prepare themselves by developing new skills, focusing on complex tasks, building soft skills, learning from customer interactions, and embracing AI-powered tools.

the advancements in artificial intelligence have undoubtedly impacted various professions, some more than others. Many jobs that once required human skills and intelligence are now being automated, leading to concerns about job security and the future of work.

However, it is essential to note that while AI may be able to perform certain tasks more efficiently, it cannot replicate the entirety of human skills and experiences. Many professions require creativity, emotional intelligence, and critical thinking, which are not currently replicable by AI.

Therefore, while some professions may be on the brink of being replaced by AI, it is unlikely that AI will entirely replace human workers in all areas. Instead, we may see a shift in job roles and responsibilities, with more emphasis on skills that cannot be replicated by AI.

As we continue to develop and integrate AI into our work processes, it is crucial to consider the potential impact on human workers. It is important to invest in education and training programs to ensure that workers have the skills they need to adapt to the changing job market. Additionally, policymakers and businesses must work together to create a sustainable and equitable future of work, where both humans and AI can thrive.